D0513472

DESTINATION *Sydney*

MAGNIFICENT PANORAMIC VIEWS

PANOGRAPHS®
PUBLISHING PTY LTD

Famous for its beaches, its harbour, its buildings and its history, Sydney is a city of spectacular variety and beauty. Its harsh beginnings as a British convict colony have long been eclipsed by its transformation into one of the world's great metropolises, blessed with one of the finest natural locations on the planet. Built against the backdrop of the rugged Blue Mountains and honeycombed by waterways, the city is today a delightful mix of spectacular landscape and urban living, and a firm tourist favourite!

For many Sydneysiders, pride of place is given to the city's magnificent harbour. The water cuts through the city like a ribbon of blue, broken into a myriad of tiny bays, sparkling with light at every touch of the sun. In the centre rises the world-famous Harbour Bridge – like an enormous coat-hanger – and just across the water loom the smooth white sails of Sydney's iconic Opera House. The inner city itself is a joyful blend of new and old: historic sandstone buildings and quaint terrace houses merge into a vibrant CBD and an abundance of entertainment venues. Further afield lie countless enclaves of diverse culture and lifestyle, from the prosperous 'North Shore' to the sprawling cosmopolitan south and west, and the sun-soaked beaches of the eastern coast.

Captured here in glorious colour by world-renowned photographer Ken Duncan, Destination Sydney is a tour in miniature of a remarkable city.

Nothing should be prized more highly than the value of each day.

Sunrise reveals a blue-washed sea-pool at Newport Beach. One of many ocean pools along Sydney's Pacific coast, this shot illustrates the simple architecture behind much of the city's outdoor lifestyle. In Sydney the gifts of nature are everywhere.

TITLE PAGE
Sydney Opera House

PREVIOUS PAGE
Sun seekers, Bronte Beach

THIS PAGE
Newport Beach Baths

In stillness,
we begin to see
our true reflection.

The sheltered waters of Pittwater,
seen here in the first light of morning,
provide a perfect safe haven for countless boats.
On weekends and holidays, the yachts' billowing
sails transform the waterway into a giant playground.

THIS PAGE
Sunrise Reflections, Bayview

NEXT PAGE
Sydney Harbour aerial

*In the right light,
at the right time,
everything is
extraordinary.*

*This little island – off Mrs Macquaries Point – once
housed recalcitrant convicts in solitary confinement.
It was fortified against a possible Russian attack
during the Crimean War. Today it haunts tourists
with its memories of a bygone age.*

Fort Denison, Sydney Harbour

*Time and tide
wait for no man.*

THIS PAGE
Sunrise, North Curl Curl

NEXT PAGE
Bondi Beach aerial

*If life
is all about
the journey,
then why rush?*

Darling Harbour boasts everything from a
spectacular aquarium and the Australian National
Maritime Museum to relaxed cafés, restaurants and
tourist arcades. Here, a ferry from yesteryear –
transformed into a floating restaurant – lounges in
the bright sun-soaked surrounds of Cockle Bay.

PREVIOUS PAGE
Bondi Beach

THIS PAGE
Darling Harbour

*A man's dreams
are an index
to his greatness.*

Built out of sandstone, with its ornate Victorian
façade, the Town Hall (left) is one of Sydney's
best-known landmarks. On the right, with its
green domes, is the lavish Byzantine-inspired
Queen Victoria Building, completed in 1898.

THIS PAGE
Sydney Town Hall and Queen Victoria Building

NEXT PAGE
Eastern Suburbs aerial

*Never get so busy
making a living
that you forget
to make a life.*

Protected by a shark net, this eastern suburbs
beach looks out upon the magnificence of
Sydney Harbour – as white-sailed yachts sail away
in the blue. The harbour hides many delightful
curves of sand in its abundant bays and inlets.

THIS PAGE
Shark Beach, Nielsen Park

*In every outthrust headland,
in every curving beach,
in every grain of sand there
is the story of the earth.*

*Seen from the Barrenjoey Headland, Palm Beach
appears as an empty expanse of spectacular surf
and sand. Life is more relaxed in these far northern
suburbs, where the rhythm of the ocean brings
an ageless sense of calm.*

THIS PAGE
Palm Beach and Barrenjoey Headland

NEXT PAGE
Pastel Sunrise, Freshwater Beach

I know of no pleasure deeper than that which comes from contemplating the natural world.

A moody sea breaks over the rocks at Maroubra, its emotive impact heightened by an ethereal grey and yellow sky. Not all days are good for swimming along Sydney's eastern fringe, but all have their own unique glory.

PREVIOUS PAGE
Sunrise, Sydney Harbour

THIS PAGE
Mahon Pool, Maroubra

33

*Praise is like sunlight
to the human spirit:
we cannot flower
and grow without it.*

*In contrast to the scene on the previous page,
this photograph reveals the ocean in a magnificent
moment of stillness. The sun appears like a stream
of liquid gold as the Coogee baths reflect
the soft cloud patterns overhead.*

THIS PAGE
Coogee Sea Pool

NEXT PAGE
Manly aerial

*Man is free
at the moment
he wishes to be.*

For Sydneysiders, fishing is something of
a city-wide passion, with thousands throwing lines
from beaches, rocks, riverbanks and boats.
Even Manly, one of Sydney's most popular beaches,
provides an idyllic fishing spot at sunrise – and large
fish may still be caught.

THIS PAGE
Sunrise, Manly Beach

*Eighty percent
of success
is showing up.*

Captured from the air, this surf carnival at
Freshwater Beach reveals its various elements
like a map: the crowds, tents, boats and sea.
Sydney is famous for its lifeguards.
At events like these they test and hone their skills.

THIS PAGE
Freshwater Beach aerial

NEXT PAGE
Sydney Harbour Bridge Climb

If you don't know where you are going, how can you expect to get there?

NEXT PAGE
Sydney Celebration

*Every New Years Eve, the Sydney Harbour Bridge
and its surrounds explode with fiery colour
to welcome the coming year. The pin-lights of the city
show that hundreds of thousands have stayed up
to watch this world famous spectacle!*

THIS PAGE
The Spit

Harbour Reflections, Sydney

DESTINATION SYDNEY
First published 2007
by Panographs® Publishing Pty Ltd
ABN 21 050 235 606
PO Box 3015, Wamberal,
NSW, 2260, Australia
Telephone +61 2 4367 6777
Email: panos@kenduncan.com

©2007, Panographs® Publishing
Pty Ltd. This publication is
copyright. Other than for the
purposes of and subject to
the conditions prescribed
under the Copyright Act 1968
(Commonwealth of Australia), no
part of it in any form or by any
means (electronic, mechanical,
microcopying, photocopying,
recording or otherwise) may be
reproduced, stored in a retrieval
system or transmitted without
prior written permission of
Panographs® Publishing Pty Ltd.
Panographs® is a registered
trademark of the Ken Duncan
Group Pty Limited.

Photography and text
by Ken Duncan
©2007 Divine Guidance P/L
Designed by Good Catch Design
Reprographics by CFL Print Studio
Printed and bound in China

The National Library of Australia
Cataloguing-in-Publication entry:
Destination Sydney:
magnificent panoramic views.
ISBN 9780977573028 (hbk.).
1. Sydney (N.S.W.) - Description
and travel - Pictorial works.
I. Duncan, Ken.
919.44100222

To view the range of Ken Duncan's
panoramic Limited Edition Prints
visit our Galleries:

- 414 The Entrance Road, Erina
  Heights, NSW
  Telephone +61 2 4367 6701
- 73 George Street, The Rocks,
  Sydney, NSW
  Telephone +61 2 9241 3460
- Shop U6 Southgate,
  Melbourne, Vic
  Telephone +61 3 9686 8022
- Shop 14 Hunter Valley
  Gardens Village,
  Broke Road, Pokolbin, NSW
  Telephone +61 2 4998 6711

VISIT THE KEN DUNCAN GALLERY ONLINE: www.kenduncan.com